THE METROPOLIS OF TOMORROW

BY

Hugh Ferriss

DOVER PUBLICATIONS, INC.
MINEOLA, NEW YORK

Bibliographical Note

This Dover edition, first published in 2005, is an unabridged republication of the work originally published in 1929 by Ives Washburn, Publisher, New York.

Library of Congress Cataloging-in-Publication Data

Ferriss, Hugh, 1889–
    The metropolis of tomorrow / Hugh Ferriss.
        p. cm.
    Originally published: New York : Ives Washburn, 1929.
    ISBN 0-486-43727-2 (pbk.)
    1. Ferriss, Hugh, 1889——Themes, motives. 2. Cities and towns—
Forecasting. 3. Skyscrapers in art. 4. Visionary architecture. I. Title.
NA9085.F47F47 2005
724.6—dc22
                                                                2004056233

Manufactured in the United States of America
Dover Publications, Inc., 31 East 2nd Street, Mineola, N.Y. 11501

To those men who, as Commissioners of
numerous American municipalities, are
laboring upon the economic, legal,
social and engineering aspects
of City Planning, this book—
which aspires to add a
visual element to
the endeavor—is
respectfully
inscribed

FOREWORD

REALIZING, as the author does, how dubious a business is that of "Prophecy", he at once disclaims any assumption of the prophet's robe. How are the cities of the future really going to look? Heaven only knows! Certainly the author has had no thought, while sketching these visualizations, that he had been vouchsafed any Vision. He will only claim that these studies are not entirely random shots in the dark, and that his foreshadowings and interpretations spring from something at least more trustworthy than personal phantasy.

The fact is, these drawings have for the greater part been made in leisure moments during the fifteen years or so in which it has been the author's daily task to work, as Illustrator or Consulting Designer, on the typical buildings which our contemporary architectural firms are erecting, day by day, in the larger cities. He should not be charged with waywardness if he has sought, during this period, to discover some of the trends which underlie the vast miscellany of contemporary building, or wondered (in drawings) where these trends may possibly, or even probably, lead. And he may be indulged if he has occasionally stepped aside from the technical limitations of current work to freely imagine a "Metropolis of Tomorrow"—choosing, as his cues, those tendencies which seem, to him, best to promise the ultimate embodiment, in structural forms, of certain human values.

This collection falls, accordingly, into three sections. In the first are pictured some of the more significant structures which already exist (or which are rising as this book goes to press) with many of which the cosmopolitan reader is already familiar. The names of the buildings and their designers are given; the group is presented as a matter-of-fact record of existing conditions.

In the second section, a number of the principal trends, underlying and manifesting themselves in the existing situation, are isolated for a brief pictorial study. At the same time, consideration is given to proposals, now being offered by various experts and commonly discussed in the architectural field, for the development or modification of these trends. A visualization is presented of the cities which would come into existence were these trends, or these propositions, carried forward.

In the third section, certain of these influences are particularly selected and brought together in glimpses of an imaginary Metropolis concerning whose true raison d'etre a few remarks will be ventured later on. . .

CONTENTS

ACKNOWLEDGEMENT

For the kind coöperation shown in permitting reproduction of certain of these drawings, the author records his thanks to the following: Corbett, Harrison and McMurray, Architects; Ramond Hood, Architect; Holabird and Root, Architects; Mauram, Russell and Crowell, Architects; The American Institute of Steel Construction, Inc.; The Lehigh Portland Cement Company; The Chanin Construction Company; The J. L. Hudson Company; Mr. Louis L. Horch; The Daily News; The St. Louis Post Dispatch.

ILLUSTRATIONS

PART THREE — An Imaginary Metropolis.

CITIES OF TODAY

PART ONE

A FIRST IMPRESSION of the contemporary city—let us say, the view of New York from the work-room in which most of these drawings were made—is not unlike the sketch on the opposite page. This, indeed, is to the author the familiar morning scene. But there are occasional mornings when, with an early fog not yet dispersed, one finds oneself, on stepping onto the parapet, the spectator of an even more nebulous panorama. Literally, there is nothing to be seen but mist; not a tower has yet been revealed below, and except for the immediate parapet rail (dark and wet as an ocean liner's) there is not a suggestion of either locality or solidity for the coming scene. To an imaginative spectator, it might seem that he is perched in some elevated stage box to witness some gigantic spectacle, some cyclopean drama of forms; and that the curtain has not yet risen.

There is a moment of curiosity, even for those who have seen the play before, since in all probability they are about to view some newly arisen steel skeleton, some tower or even some street which was not in yesterday's performance. And to one who had not been in the audience before—to some visitor from another land or another age—there could not fail to be at least a moment of wonder. What apocalypse is about to be revealed? What is its setting? And what will be the purport of this modern metropolitan drama?

Soon, somewhere off in the mist, a single lofty highlight of gold appears: the earliest beam is upon the tip of the Metropolitan Tower. A moment later, a second: the gilded apex of the New York Life Building. And then, in due succession the other architectural principals lift their pinnacles into vision: the Brooklyn skyscraper group, the Municipal building, the Woolworth. The promised spectacle is apparently at least to include some lofty presences . . .

But a subtle differentiation is beginning to occur below in the monotone of gray; vertical lines, but a degree more luminous, appear on all sides; the eastern facades of the city grow pale with light. As mysteriously as though being created, a Metropolis appears.

Obviously, we can now conclude, it is to be a city of closely juxtaposed verticals. And, indeed, it is not until considerably later, when the mists have been completely dispersed, that there is revealed far below—through bridge and river and avenue—the presence of any horizontal base whatever for these cloud-capped towers.

One further discovery remains to be made: on a close scrutiny of the streets, certain minute, moving objects can be unmistakably distinguished. The city apparently contains, away down there—human beings!

The discovery gives one pause. Between the colossal inanimate forms and those mote-like creatures darting in and out among their foundations, there is such a contrast, such discrepancy in scale, that certain questions force their attention on the mind.

What is the relation between these two? Are those tiny specks the actual intelligences of the situation, and this towered mass something which, as it were, those ants have marvelously excreted?

· 15 ·

Or are these masses of steel and glass the embodiment of some blind and mechanical force that has imposed itself, as though from without, on a helpless humanity?

At first glance, one might well imagine the latter. Nevertheless, there is but one view which can be taken; there is but one fact that can—in these pages, at least—serve as our criterion. The drama which, from this balcony, we have been witnessing is, first and foremost, a human drama. Those vast architectural forms are only a stage set. It is those specks of figures down there below who are, in reality, the principals of the play.

But what influences have these actors and this stage reciprocally upon one another? How perfectly or imperfectly have the actors expressed themselves in their constructions—how well have the architects designed the set? And how great is the influence which the architectural background exercises over the actors—and is it a beneficient one?

I have just said that the human being is the Principal, and it is indeed true that the human values are here the principal values. Yet it must be realized, as one gazes over this multiform and miscellaneous city, that the builders must at least have been lacking in the two attributes usually assigned to principals—clear sense of the situation and manifest ability to control it.

Is the set well designed? Indeed, it is not designed at all! It is true that in individual fragments of the set here and there—in individual buildings—we see the conscious hand of the architect. But in speaking, as we are, of the city as a whole, it is impossible to say that it did more than come to be built; we must admit that, as a whole, it is not work of conscious design.

And nevertheless it is a faithful expression! Architecture never lies. Architecture invariably expresses its Age correctly. Admire or condemn as you may, yonder skyscrapers faithfully express both the characteristic structural skill and the characteristic urge—for money; yonder tiers of apartments represent the last word in scientific ingenuity and the last word but one in desire for physical comfort.

As regards the effect which the "set" is having upon the actors: it is unquestionably enormous. I am not referring to the effect of the physical conveniences (or inconveniences) which it provides—and of which we are all acutely aware—but to another kind of influence which is none the less direct and potent for being difficult to define. It is well known and generally admitted that a few people are especially sensitive to the element of design; but a more serious and equally indubitable fact is that the character of the architectural forms and spaces which all people habitually encounter are powerful agencies in determining the nature of their thoughts, their emotions and their actions, however unconscious of this they may be.

The boy whose habitual outlook was over wide, open plains and the boy who habitually dwelt among the mountains have received impressions lasting for life from these forms and have become, in consequence, utterly different types of men. What is true of plains and mountains is no less true of architectural forms; everybody is influenced by the house he inhabits, be it harmonious or mean, by the streets in which he walks and by the buildings among which he finds himself.

Are not the inhabitants of most of our American cities continually glancing at the rising masses of office or apartment buildings whose thin coating of architectural confectionery disguises, but does not alter, the fact that they were fashioned to meet not so much the human needs of the occupants as the financial appetites of the property owners? Do we not traverse, in our daily walks, districts which are stupid and miscellaneous rather than logical or serene—and move, day long, through an absence of viewpoint, vista, axis, relation or plan? Such an environment silently but relentlessly impresses its qualities upon the human psyche.

The contemplation of the actual Metropolis as a whole cannot but lead us at last to the realization of a human population unconsciously reacting to forms which came into existence without conscious design.

A hope, however, may begin to define itself in our minds. May there not yet arise, perhaps in another generation, architects who, appreciating the influence unconsciously received, will learn consciously to direct it?

But we may postpone more general conclusions until we have examined, at closer view, the existing facts. Let us go down into the streets . . .

GOING DOWN INTO THE STREETS of a modern city must seem—to the new-comer, at least—a little like Dante's descent into Hades. Certainly so unacclimated a visitor would find, in the dense atmosphere, in the kaleidoscopic sights, the confused noise and the complex physical contacts, something very reminiscent of the lower realms.

The condemned—that is to say, the habitual city dwellers—seem to be used to it and to take it for granted; yet one occasionally wonders if some subtle alteration, of which they themselves are unaware, is not occurring in their facial expressions, their postures, gestures, movements, tones of voice—in short, their total behavior!

We usually feel that the traffic situation is getting a little worse every day. Certainly every year, if not quite every day, it is becoming perceptibly several degrees more congested and is now rapidly approaching the point of public danger. As the avenues and streets of a city are nothing less than its arteries and veins, we may well ask what doctor would venture to promise bodily health if he knew that the blood circulation was steadily growing more congested!

With a very few exceptions (such as the Superhighway project of Detroit) no design for urban traffic is now being proposed that can truly be called masterly. This is the problem of problems that must be comprehended if we are adequately to visualize the future city. Nevertheless, we must postpone it for a moment and give our attention first of all to the architectural structures of present-day cities. We shall not be going far out of our way, since the buildings of a city—especially as to their cubic contents—are the determining factor in its traffic congestion; and a further advantage lies in the fact that buildings exhibit, although the traffic situation does not, the deliberate hand of the designer. By scrutinizing one by one, some of the outstanding buildings of the country, we shall be able to get some clue to what our more influential designers are about; and after determining the trends their designs indicate, we shall have the strands for our pattern of the city of the future. Let us, then, glance at a few of the more significant structures in various of the larger cities. . . .

THE CITY AT NIGHT
Descent into the streets.

IMPRESSIONS OF THE EXISTING CITY which have so far been mentioned are not, of course, local to New York. Many watchers have, in similar mood, looked down on Pittsburgh at dawn; there was, for instance, the hour during which Town Planner Frederick Bigger analyzed the panorama which unfolded itself beneath us across the Monongahela. Waiting, on Twin Peaks, to watch, with Architect T. L. Pflueger, the whole of San Francisco in deepening twilight, similar queries arose to mind. And Chicago seen at night (at least on a September night which I well remember) brought up identical questions as to the nature and significance of the metropolis.

As our first example of an individual building, a St. Louis structure is shown. This is not because of a native's enthusiasm but because—in our inquiry into the contributory value of contemporary architects—this building will provide us with an encouraging start.

Here, an architectural form, unique in its locality, came into existence not as an indirect result of some legal or economic cause, but as the direct result of a bold stroke on the part of its designers. The designers, moreover, were quite obviously moved by a consideration of what might be immediately accomplished in the way of human convenience and health.

At the time this building was erected, St. Louis had no building regulation which required or even suggested this set-back type of structure. The rank and file of previous buildings had been of the familiar box-like shape. The architects in this case were therefore quite free to follow the convention: they could easily have thus supplied the owners with the required cubage and, in short, have performed all the obligations usually demanded of architects. It is apparent, however, that they foresaw that this set-back type of structure, while giving all the interior space specified, would allow for floor plans considerably more convenient and agreeable to the individual occupants; would allow decidedly more light and air to their neighbors across the streets; and could be designed—as the conventional cube-like structure cannot be designed—to express the concepts of individuality, ascension and summit.

The proposal of the designers was in due course appreciated by their clients, and, after the usual investigation, permit to build was issued. But the true contributory value lies, perhaps, in this: in a very short time after the completion of the building, regulations were proposed and incorporated into the local building code which not only permitted but approved such forms.

Since we intend to build up our image of the "Metropolis of Tomorrow" from existing material, we may take, as one of our ingredients, the fact that a sound innovation of idea may, in a surprisingly short time, become embodied.

THE TELEPHONE BUILDING, ST. LOUIS
Mauran, Russell and Crowell, Architects.
I. R. Timlin, Associate Architect.

ANOTHER CONTEMPORARY PROJECT which like the Telephone Building, may provide a pointer for future use, is the St. Louis Plaza. Unlike the Telephone Building, however, the Plaza points, not to accomplishment on the part of the individual designer, but to an accomplishment resulting from the collaboration of numerous designers.

It is true, by the way, that the Plaza is not a fully accomplished fact at the present moment. Since, however, it has been financially assured through the voting of the necessary bond issues, since certain major parts are actually constructed and the whole project is outlined definitely in blue-prints, it becomes possible to prepare authentic visualizations. This project involves the demolition of numerous city blocks—a great area previously occupied by totally insignificant buildings. The clearing thus made lies, however, between such outstanding civic structures as Public Library, City Hall and Municipal Courts building. Not only are these important centers thus brought into clear view of one another, but the plaza which they now front becomes the site of other major, and much needed public buildings—the whole being embellished with sculpture and formal gardening. The net result is to provide this city with what so many cities lack; a plainly apparant nucleus.

It is natural that in such generally important projects, a problem is encountered in the selection of the directing architects. Everyone knows how often civic building programs show the hand of the politician rather than that of the designer. In this case, however, it was predetermined that the personnel of the architectural commission was to be elected by vote of the local chapter of the American Institute of Architects. The promise of a truly professional character was thus made, which has, on the whole, been satisfactorily fulfilled. But even with civic projects in the hands of admittedly distinguished architects, a question arises. Will we ever get, as fruit of the collaboration of many minds, those startling satisfactory results, which are occasionally produced by the individual mind working alone? The visualist, whose commission is to analize, assemble and depict, as one project, all the contributory ideas of a large commission of architects, must often find himself at conferences where it is difficult—because of the clamor of minor variations—to discover any major theme. Indeed, one occasionally wonders if the proceedings of some architectural conferences do not defy any analysis—save, perhaps, that of the professional psychologist! The fact remains, however, that the scope of certain civic projects is so great that some sort of collaboration is essential; furthermore, as time passes, the scope of such projects will only increase and collaboration will be only the more essential.

The St. Louis Plaza suggests, perhaps, that a collaboration may indeed occur without, as a necessary concomitant, absence of a strong and unified result.

THE ST. LOUIS PLAZA
George D. Barnett, Inc.—T. P. Barnett Company—Preston J. Bradshaw—Helsen Stellor, Hirsch & Watson—William B. Ittner—Klipstein & Rathman—La Beaume & Klein—Mauran, Rusell & Crowell—Associated Architects.

CHICAGO, in the last decade, has reared towers which, in pictorial interest, rival any of the metropolitan centers of the East. We have, of course, been long familiar with the sheer façade of the city which faces the lake across Michigan Boulevard; but a formation of quite different character has recently begun to crystallize definitely about the winding line of the river. Walking by night along Wacker Drive—or under it—a series of startling compositions revolve before the spectator.

Judging by certain projects which already exist in blue-print form, there will soon be another distinguished development fronting the newly made lands along the lake front. Indeed, the whole current tone of the city's structural development is a good omen for the projected international exposition of 1933. This project should be noted on these pages because—to base a prediction on the personnel of the architectural commission as well as on the designs which they are already formulating—this exposition will prove to be not only an epitome of our most modern architectural developments but also a herald of future actual developments.

An adequate suggestion of the most recent trend in Chicago is conveyed by the Board of Trade building whose strong, ascending mass stands out strikingly against the older buildings which are about it.

THE CHICAGO BOARD OF TRADE
Holabird & Root, Architects.

ANOTHER CHICAGO STRUCTURE which contributes to any bird's-eye view of the American scene, is the Tribune tower. This building is an admirable monument of an unusually significant architectural competition.

It will be recalled that the Chicago TRIBUNE conducted a competition whose avowed purpose was to produce the "most beautiful office building in the world." It spent over a hundred thousand dollars in assembling and rewarding contributory ideas.

The superlative need not be taken too seriously; but the fact remains that a handsome invitation was issued to contribute an element of beauty to a commercial structure, and that competent responses were received from architects the world over. Nearly three hundred designs were submitted, representing twenty-three countries.

The competition proved influential in more ways than one. The more significant designs, published in book form, constituted a valuable collection of modern trends; it gave pictorial point to many a discussion, and found echoes, here and there, in subsequent building. The design which was awarded the second prize proved to be the passport to the American scene of Architect Eliel Saarinen, of Finland, whose presence has already influenced our most recent buildings and whose decided point of view may, before long, influence our larger civic projects. Finally, the tower which was actually erected added a gratifying silhouette to the lake front and has, without doubt, proved an inspiration to many.

THE CHICAGO TRIBUNE BUILDING
John Mead Howells and Raymond M. Hood, Architects.

THE RADIATOR BUILDING, in New York City, has one undeniable virtue: it has undoubtedly provoked more arguments among laymen on the subject of architectural values than any other structure in the country.

Clearly seen, as it is, from across Bryant Park, or glimpsed from Fifth Avenue (with its bold gold crown rising impertinently above the respectable Library), it stops people, daily, in their tracks; they exclaim how much they like, or dislike, its emphatic form and its radical color scheme.

It is, by the way, of some interest to compare it with the Tribune tower, just seen in Chicago, since the same designer had a hand in each. Those critics who found a sentimental historic association in the stone-covered steel buttresses atop the Tribune, would scarcely find anything at all reminiscent in the later, and bolder, tower on Bryant Park.

Unhappily, the gold which crowns the tower,—and which can be seen gleaming from as far away as Staten Island,—cannot be reproduced in this illustration, which pays its respects only to the black. In the black and white rendition one can, indeed, consider the form which, in the structure itself, is distinctly virile. Yet it is probably the color contrast of the building which gives pause and provokes the valuable discussion. The Radiator building is, in this respect at least, decidedly an experiment. Here is a point to remember when we come to sketch the future city—there are at least a few trained and experienced architects who have no fear of experimentation.

THE RADIATOR BUILDING
Raymond M. Hood, Architect.

A STRANGE YET MAJESTIC FORM began to loom against the New York horizon in 1922. It was something like the arrival, in Lilliputia, of the vast stranger. People paused in the streets. A hubbub arose amongst the scholarly lilliputian critics. The newcomer was "uncouth," "uncivilized": it lacked "style," "scale," "taste."

It is interesting to recall how nervous was the reception; to remember how, during the ensuing two years, the litmus paper of popular opinion shifted its unstable hue; how the Medal of Honor was finally awarded; and how so many of yesterday's critics have now persuaded themselves that they liked it from the start.

The Shelton was one of the first of the very large buildings to be erected after the enacting of the local "Zoning Laws"; that is to say, it is one of the early examples of the "set-back" type of structure. The occasion, perhaps, was the very first on which an architect, confronted by those novel limitations, was not embarrassed.

What a struggle some of the designers made to force into the new "envelope" the stylistic concepts with which their minds were filled! In this case, it would appear that the architect faced, without distaste, the volumes with which he was permitted to deal; and modeled, with a single broad tool, the mass which would most simply fill his space.

There is, in the building itself, something reminiscent of the mountain. Many people choose it as a residence, or frequent its upper terraces, because——known or unknown to them——it evokes that undefinable sense of satisfaction which man ever finds on the slope of the pyramid or the mountainside.

The Shelton is already encircled by more recent buildings which equal it only in height; but there remains at least one point of vantage from which its massive bulk can, if only transitorily, still be glimpsed.

THE SHELTON HOTEL
Arthur Loomis Harmon, Architect.

THE NEW STIMULUS which the Zoning Laws gave to architectural design immediately produced another interesting reaction, on the part of another architect, in the Belden project.

The sketch makes no attempt to delineate a finished building, but deals solely with mass. It was thus simplified in order better to illustrate the novel elements of such a design.

It will be recalled that until quite recently, the typical commercial façade was designed in three main parts—base, shaft and crowning member. For years it went without saying that an architect must enclose the first two or three stories in an "order"—columns or pilasters; that above this, the façade was to be permitted to express the internal facts in a straightforward fenestration—until the uppermost two or three stories were reached; whereupon, convention again demanded the row of columns engaged (but not married!) to the building and a gigantic, expensive and absolutely useless cornice.

In the Belden design we again discern three main stages—but how different from the conventional triad! They are not theoretical, applied and two-dimensional,—but three dimensional, inherent and self-evident. There is the main body of the building which rises sheerly from the ground—the transitional stage in which the mass breaks, recedes and diversifies—and the lofty tower into which it finally resolves.

THE BELDEN PROJECT
Corbett, Harrison and McMurray, Architects.

THE FORM which appeared, in comparatively simple outline, in the Belden project is found carried to a more mature conclusion, by the same architect, in the Master building on Riverside Drive. The three main divisions of mass are still evident, but their interrelation is here more carefully studied and the modeling throughout is more fully developed.

This structure presents more than one innovation which it will be well to remember when it comes to sketching the city of the future. As a matter of fact, what usually attracts the attention of passers-by on the Drive is the unusual placing of the windows—at the very corners of the structure. Upon some, this produces an uneasy impression—for the simple reason that their preconceptions of structural strength are based on the masonry structures they have previously seen. To others, this disposition of windows is immediately satisfying—since they have acquainted themselves with the elements of steel construction and know that this corner treatment is, in steel, structurally sound. The glazed corner is, indeed, justified by the structural fact that it is, in addition, desirable: it provides the corner room with an unusual degree of light and air as well as a sense of spaciousness which will prove surprising to the average city dweller.

Another item worth remembering is that the brick, with which the walls are faced, instead of being the usual monotone throughout, is graded, in color, from dark at the base to light at the top; it suggests a kind of growth, and it is not, indeed, entirely fantastic to speak of a building as something which has grown.

THE MASTER BUILDING
Corbett, Harrison and McMurray, Architects.
Sugarman & Berger, Associate Architects.

THOSE WHO RECALL the appearance of the Waldorf-Astoria hotel will find, in the office building which is about to take its place, a vivid illustration of the contemporary trend in architecture.

To some, no doubt, the heavy masonry arches and the mosque-like domes of the older structure will seem the more appealing—standing, for them, as it must, for the familiar charm of older days and presenting no challenging or disturbing thought.

Yet many will experience a strong emotion in the presence of the vast steps and the sheer ascending planes of structure now arising. In its forthright structural simplicity, its scale, and its power, it definitely announces the coming of a new order.

THE WALDORF-ASTORIA OFFICE BUILDING
Shreve, Lamb and Harmon, Architects.

Hugh Ferriss

"A CIRCULAR SPACE, 150 feet in circumference,—to be enclosed by a wall of black glass which rises, unbroken by any windows, to a black glass ceiling; in the center of a brass-inlaid floor, a cup-shaped well from which light—the sole illumination of the room — is to stream. Bathed in this light, a ten-foot terrestrial globe is to revolve — its even revolutions reflected darkly in the night-like ceiling above."

The foregoing specification might seem to point, perhaps, to a hall dedicated to some high scientific or even religious idea: it would scarcely be taken to refer to the entrance lobby of a newspaper and office building. Yet just this lobby, as described, stands within a stone's throw of Grand Central Terminal.

Why is so bizarre a design included in so utilitarian a building? Has it merely a publicity value? What effect, if any, will it have upon the thousands of people who hurry in and out every day?

It can scarcely be doubted that the sight of it will give them pause, if only momentarily. Is it possible that as they glance for an instant at a miniature revolving in a black glass room, they may experience at least passing realization of the situation of their own planet—revolving, at that very instant, in the black crystal of space?

Would it not be surprising if the sense of large actualities, which is often lacking in the words of both contemporary scientists and churchmen, should be brought to us in the wordless device of an architect!

LOBBY, THE DAILY NEWS BUILDING
John Mead Howells and Raymond M. Hood, Architects.

AN IMPRESSIVE TOWER—a beautiful subject for the draughtsman; not to be counted among buildings actually erected—but to be included in this survey because it was one of the last conceptions of a designer who, throughout all his works, greatly influenced the direction of American architecture: the late Bertram Grosvenor Goodhue.

This structure was proposed for a site adjoining Madison Square Garden; as may be guessed from its appearance, it was to house, on the main floor, a great auditorium (in fact, a church) and above this, the huge shaft containing offices was to rise some thousand feet from the ground.

There are critics who will say that it seems of stone rather than of steel, and they may not add that the buttressed corners (which contain elevator shafts and stairways) were designed in disregard of the financial value of corner offices. All the same, and in spite of the excellent case of the critic, the tower itself produces in the spectator a strong emotional impression—exactly the impression, by the way, which the gifted architect intended to convey.

THE CONVOCATION TOWER
Bertrand Grosvenor Goodhue, Architect.

DETROIT is an exceptional city in this respect among others: in the matter of traffic, it has not only formulated, but begun to materialize, a system of superhighways conceived in dimensions of the future. Here is an instance in which the City of Tomorrow is comprehended and definitely foreshadowed by the City of Today. The "Master Plan," so called, embraces and is supported not only by Detroit, but by three adjoining counties, including twenty separate municipalities. Ample provisions are made for the movement of the great concentrations of industrial workers, ·as well as for their adequate transportation between urban and suburban districts.

With the broad avenues and express highways thus assured, which are essential to free circulation, attention turns to the other great factor of city planning; that is to say, the kind of buildings which must rise along the avenues. For obviously, cities of the future will require not only increased traffic space, but a balanced building program, as well.

Today, the buildings of Detroit can scarcely be said to represent any balance. In a city which has grown so rapidly, to such great proportions, it is only to be expected that we should find, as we do, extensive areas of low, mediocre, frame structures. But side by side with them, there are new towering buildings, three of which are illustrated herewith; and these are undoubtedly the forerunners of the future city.

THE GREATER PENOBSCOT BUILDING
Smith, Hinchman and Grylls, Architects.

AN UNUSUAL COÖPERATION on the part of owner, builder and collaborating artists, with the architect himself (if we may judge by the latter's published statements), must have contributed to the remarkably through result embodied in the Fisher Building. This coöperation is, perhaps, a factor which we shall need in upbuilding the future city. Yet the fact remains that the strong qualities which this structure preeminently exhibits are precisely those which caused the rapid rise in the architectural field of this individual designer.

The accompanying sketch indicates only a portion of the whole Fisher project; a second mass is to companion the one shown; both of them flank a central tower which will rise to considerably greater heights.

THE FISHER BUILDING
Albert Kahn, Architect.

A SPECIES OF TOWER-BUILDINGS—rather than an assortment of unrelated individual towers—seems to be appearing on the contemporary architectural scene.

The structure here illustrated is, obviously, quite distinct from the Panhellenic Tower in New York, just as the Panhellenic Tower is, obviously, quite distinct from the Radiator Building. Yet despite their individual differences, it is apparent that they constitute, on the whole, a single architectural species.

Their community lies, perhaps, in some similarity of proportion, or silhouette, or vertical movement, or organic structure. In any case, there is clear indication that we are in the presence of something more momentous than a sporadic individual; this uprising is one of truly great proportions!

DAVID STOTT BUILDING
Donaldson & Meier, Architects.

THE LONELY TOWER OF LOS ANGELES is, in itself, a striking form. One approaches it, from below, with lively interest. One enters——takes elevator to the observation gallery——and here observes——how monotonous are all the other architectural masses in the city!

It appears that the local Zoning Laws set a definite height limit to the taller business buildings. As this height is moderate, almost all owners build in practically all their areas, to the legal limit. The result, obviously, is a series of cube-like structures standing side to side——offering to the spectator (and the designer) only a two-dimensional façade.

There is a number of beautiful façades in Los Angeles; but if an architect is to produce a success out of a single façade, he must use ingenuity——and ingenuity is, to a designer, one of the smaller tools. With the Los Angeles type of regulation, the larger tools of the architect must remain unused.

So, for the time being, the City Hall (permitted by a very special legal dispensation) continues to stand in solitary grandeur. Later on the human life which pulsates so youthfully about its base will crystallize itself in architectural forms and provide a more vividly sculptured milieu. In the meantime, there are the vivid hills——to which the tower, perhaps, addresses itself.

THE LOS ANGELES MUNICIPAL TOWER
John Parkinson, John C. Austin,
Albert C. Martin, Associated Architects.

OF THE 377 SKYSCRAPERS more than twenty stories high, which stand in the United States in 1929, 188 rise within the narrow limits of New York City. Fifteen of these are over five hundred feet tall; and of these fifteen, two—those illustrated on the opposite and the succeeding page—are exactly across the street from each other.

When excavations were begun for the earlier of these—the Chanin building—the corner of Lexington and Forty-second Street presented a fairly congested scene. True, the Commodore Hotel across the way was a rather lowly structure,—not even thirty stories high!—but Grand Central Station was immediately at hand, and the daily ebb and flow of commuters made the adjacent sidewalks black.

Nevertheless, the deep excavation was made and the lofty tower raised. The building, in itself, aroused lively interest. The architects had struck out boldly in their design; a yet bolder lobby was designed by the owners themselves; the towering mass presents an arresting spectacle when seen, in sharp perspective, from Forty-first and Park and,—when seen from the viewpoint of the present drawing—the building itself bulks large against the lurid Manhattan sky. From the uppermost floor, one gets a quite startling view across a large section of New Jersey as well as miles of the Atlantic. Yet the flag pole was scarcely being raised at this height, and added thousands of people pouring onto Forty-second and Lexington, before another great excavation was begun directly across the street. . . .

THE CHANIN BUILDING
Sloan and Robertson, Architects.
Chanin Construction Company, Engineers.

THE EXCAVATION ACROSS THE STREET proved to be the beginning of the Chrysler building which was to overtop the Chanin—rising, in fact to considerably over eight hundred feet.

In the view which is here shown, we are looking eastward, away from the city: and from this viewpoint the tower looms up freely against the low buildings of the East Side, the river and the horizontal stretches of Long Island. Were we to view it from the opposite direction, it would, however, merge into the great mass of Grand Central sky-scrapers (although its unusual terminal curve would still surmount the whole composition) and one might have some foreboding of its effect upon the congestion of Forty-second and Lexington.

It required a considerably more detailed drawing than the one at hand to delineate the many novel effects which, in this design, the architect has ingeniously produced in the fenestration, the brick work and other details which are quite apparent in the building itself; the intention in this sketch is simply to convey an impression of the extreme dimensions which are involved.

This extreme tower, however, was scarcely under way before another great excavation was begun a little farther downtown. . . .

THE CHRYSLER BUILDING
William Van Alen, Architect.

THE EXCAVATION DOWNTOWN proved to be the beginning of the Bank of the Manhattan Company Building. Located at 40 Wall Street, it rises, above the Sub-Treasury, the Morgan office and the Stock Exchange, to no less than nine hundred feet. The twelve-story building which made way for it was razed in exactly eighteen days, and even before this old structure had been demolished, the caisson foundations for the new tower had been sunk to rock.

When we consider these giant structures at close range; when we witness the ever increasing heights to which they soar and the ever increasing speed with which they are accomplished; and when we bear in mind the scientific knowledge, the boldness and the technical skill which makes them possible, we can scarcely regard the skyscraper, as such, with other than admiration not unmixed with wonder. Nevertheless, in such a bird's-eye view as we are now essaying, it becomes almost impossible to consider skyscrapers apart from their effect on their surroundings. If one thinks of the vast number of people who are housed in a single vertical column during business hours, one must go on to visualize all of them spreading out, over the immediately adjoining streets, at five in the afternoon. Indeed, it has sometimes been suggested that an architect, when designing a structure to house ten thousand souls, should be required to take it as part of his commission to see that facilities have been provided for taking them to and from their ten thousand respective homes.

Fortunately, there is already a stirring among architects in the direction of more active participation in city planning. (Oddly enough, only a few of the five hundred City Planning commissions in the country include architects). Let us terminate a brief survey of existing buildings with the hope that the abilities which designers have shown in individual projects will before long be displayed in projects of civic, or even nation-wide, import.

THE BANK OF THE MANHATTAN COMPANY BUILDING
H. Craig Severance, Architect
Starrett Brothers, Builders.

PROJECTED TRENDS

PART TWO

"THE LURE OF THE CITY" is the romantic way of phrasing it: imagination sketches the rural youth who is ever arising to his dream of "the big city"—the unformulated yet gleaming metropolis. Call it what you will: gregarious instinct or economic necessity: the primary trend, with which we must deal in any formulation of the future city, is the trend toward centralization.

The opinion is frequently and forcefully expressed, by sincere critics, that our sole hope lies, on the contrary, in decentralization. But, if by the term is meant the dispersal of large centers of population, this must be dismissed as a mere dream. For the imagination, it paints a lovely picture—just as a memory of Colonial towns is lovely; but in all that is actually going on about us, there is nothing to be seen which gives the slightest substance to it.

The first tendency, then, with which the following sketches will deal will be the tendency toward concentration. This will lead us at once to the tendency to build higher and higher structures; and we must notice, at the same time, the various proposals to care for the accompanying traffic congestion. Thereupon, we shall have to study, in our drawings, the more recent inclination to modify and vary this rising mass—exhibited in the movement to "step back" the buildings as well as in other proposals which seek, by various means, to limit or distribute volumes. In all this, we will note the growing desire for light and air, the increasing realization of the value of direct sunlight, the utilization of terraces and even the planting thereon of shrubs and trees. We should notice the tendency to assemble larger plots as bases for single towering structures. And a few lines, at least, must be drawn in reference to the development of materials—concrete, steel, glass.

But before illustrating these points, I must speak of a trend, with which it is quite impossible to deal in pictures—a trend, moreover, which will, perhaps more than any other, determine the appearance of the future city.

About the middle of June of every year, the streets of New York—especially in the vicinity of the Architects' Building—become appreciably enlivened by the presence of some five hundred young men most of whom are in the city for their first time. They have just graduated from the architectural schools of various Universities. They seek jobs! They go in—and out—of architects' reception rooms; secretaries get to know them by name, and sometimes sympathize. Judging by their behavior, as well as by their words, they are all on fire to deal with the problems which are now facing us.

But what, precisely, are they thinking? In what spirit is the coming generation of architects and city planners entering the arena?

We may safely say, in the first place, that this coming generation will move to abandon the practice, still current among designers, of evasion and deception concerning material fact. Of the architect who proposes to put a masonry column in the façade of a steel building in such a way as to suggest that it is serving as a support (when, in fact, support is provided by the steel, and the column supports nothing) they will say: "This is an untruth—as definitely as though he stated he is supporting some cause when, in fact, he is a slacker."

The whole custom of employing forms which no longer serve functions—the whole frame of mind which conceives that structural beauty can exist without truth —they will view as decadence; just as they will dismiss, as sentimentality, the notion that architectural beauty was once and for all delivered to the builders of ancient times. The employment of modern construction to support what are little more than classic or medieval stage sets, they will look upon as, at its most harmless, a minor theatrical art, but no longer as being Architecture.

On the other hand, they will without hesitation or embarrassment assemble and have before them every item of contemporary scientific research, and with these units they will build. Though the public continues, through habit, to conceive structural strength in terms of masonry, they will not continue to misinterpret, for the public's indulgence, the new language of steel; in a building where the load is carried more on the interior than the exterior column, they will not place a façade which states, falsely, that the greatest load is carried on the corners. Certainly, they will employ such materials as the recently developed forms of translucent glass over areas appropriate, not to the masonry wall, but to the steel grill. They will see in the grill itself not a means whereby to support some preconceived end, but something which is an end in itself. Briefly, they will take the architectural problem to be not the denying, disguising or superimposing upon the material fact—but the admitting, fashioning and reveling of the material fact.

Many people believe that the novel forms which are just now emerging are devoid of "beauty." Yet when the necessary time has elapsed for the younger architects to formulate their accurate statement—and for the public to comprehend accuracy—it will again appear that a new truth is inevitably attended by a new beauty.

But in addition to these material factors, we may look for the architects of Tomorrow to open what has for long, apparently, been a practically closed book—precisely that psychological importance of Architecture in the lives of people which was referred to on an earlier page.

Broadly speaking, it has been our habit to assume that a building is a complete success if it provides for the utility, convenience and health of its occupants and, in addition, presents a pleasing exterior. But this frame of mind fails to appreciate that architectural forms necessarily have other values than the utilitarian or even others than those which we vaguely call the æsthetic. Without any doubt, these same forms quite specifically influence both the emotional and the mental life of the onlooker. Designers have generally come to realize the importance of the principle stated by the late Louis Sullivan, "Form follows Function." The axiom is not weakened by the further realization that Effect follows Form.

It can be recalled that there have been periods in the past when architects must have been quite aware of the influence of Architecture and consciously employed it for a specific object. Moreover, it is precisely these periods that are still spoken of as the "great periods" of Architecture.

Of one of these—that of the early Gothic cathedrals—it has been said that those structures were reared not so much to house a particular historic church as to exert, in terms of form and space (terms safely beyond the vicissitudes of human creeds and disputations), an influence for the betterment of mankind. Certainly no one, however unused to religious emotion, can stand in certain of these designed spaces without receiving intimations of a life other, and greater, than his own. It would seem, in fact, that Architecture was here consciously employed for no less an object than the elevation and evolution of Man.

It may well be that among the coming generation of architects there are at least some who find, in such a phenomenon, a clue to the real mission of Architecture. If so, we must reckon their realization as the most important of all trends—one which will provide us, at a later day, with subject matter which no one living can yet delineate in drawings.

THE MOST POPULAR IMAGE of the Future City—to judge by what is most often expected from the draughtsman's pencil—is composed of buildings which, without any modification of their existing nature, have simply grown higher and higher. The popular mind apparently is intrigued by height, as such. A 60-story tower in New York evokes a 70-story tower in Chicago. What is more serious, a 60-story tower in New York evokes a 70-story tower directly across the street. The skyscraper is said to be America's premier architectural contribution to date, popular fancy pictures the future contribution to be rows of still higher skyscrapers; in other words, it pictures 70-story skyscrapers side by side for miles.

To the draughtsman who approaches his subject from a purely pictorial point of view, all this presents fascinating possibilities. One can easily fancy himself perched up somewhere on the hundredth floor; one looks down, at a dizzy angle, along the flanks of adjoining precipices; one is tempted to imagine the scene at night, with geometrical lights flaring in the abyss.

Yet if we relinquish the picturesque, to assume the more critical, viewpoint, do we not begin to apprehend. in this headlong ascent, something ominous? It is not a little disturbingly reminiscent of the Tower of Babel?

Certainly there are conscientious city-planners who perceive, in the present trend toward closely juxtaposed towers, a serious menace. The trend indubitably exists; and it is therefore proper, perhaps, for the draughtsman to indicate where it will lead if it is unchecked. Such drawings, however, far from being intended as an inspiration, may serve rather as a warning. "It may look like this—if nothing is done about it."

CROWDING TOWERS

TO THE SKYSCRAPING HEIGHTS of the Future City, the popular fancy usually adds something remarkable in the way of overhead traffic avenues. Scores of drawings have been produced, showing viaducts at the twentieth floor! Indeed, in some sketches, architectural values have been so completely neglected as to show the taller towers connected at their very pinnacles by a network of aerial traffic bridges which would infallibly cast their gloomy shadow permanently on the city beneath.

Following such leads, one might easily imagine, as in the accompanying drawing, that all "set-backs" of buildings have been aligned and made into automobile highways. One could drive at will across the façades of buildings, at the fifth, tenth, fifteenth or twentieth story. Automobiles below one, automobiles above one! A paradise, perhaps, for the automobile manufacturer! But for the office worker—less and less escape from the noise, the rush and the atmosphere of traffic.

Furthermore, there will be the aeroplanes. The drawing suggests tower-hangars in whose shelves they will—why not?—land neatly!

OVERHEAD TRAFFIC-WAYS

THE INCREASING TRAFFIC CONGESTION which follows in the wake of the mounting skyscraper provokes the thought that more than one traffic level, or numerous traffic levels, must indeed be eventually introduced.

To whatever extent we revise existing traffic regulations or widen avenues or cut through new streets, it appears that the circulation thus supplied is forever inadequate to the rising stream. In the minds of many experts, the only adequate solution lies in the realm of the third dimension—for instance, placing all pedestrians on a separate plane above that of the wheel traffic, and laying all rail traffic on a separate plan below. In other words, the city, as well as the countryside, would eliminate all grade crossings.

The accompanying sketch suggests what might be a first, and a modest step in this direction. The ground level is given entirely over to automobiles. Pedestrians pass overhead along arcaded walks and cross street intersections on bridges.

To introduce such a system onto Fifth Avenue or State Street or Woodward Avenue would, obviously, involve a tremendous expenditure of money. It would involve a complete and novel revision of store fronts—a shop would in fact have two main entrances: one above for the pedestrian customer and one below for the customer in his car. Yet some such innovation, however radical, seems in a long run inevitable.

PEDESTRIANS OVER WHEEL-TRAFFIC

THE CHURCH IN THE HEART OF THE CITY has of late become an interesting problem. It is a far cry back to the spired village edifice well set in its own spacious grounds, and a yet farther to the cathedral which dominated the Old World town. Trinity Church——still surrounded by its tombstones although looking directly down the axis of Wall Street——is today the unique exception.

With skyscrapers towering above the spire of the average church, and with land values also mounting beyond its income, what is that church to do? Move away from the very arena whose activities it is, avowedly, to influence? We already have several examples of another solution——the church swallowed by the skyscraper; that is to say, the Church occupies the ground floor while an office building, or an apartment house, rises around and above it.

In such situations, one is inclined to wonder whether the mood of the church permeates the offices above——or vice versa. In two or three of the examples referred to, the architect has sought (with varying success) to preserve the identity of the church by giving the whole edifice——whether it be apartments or offices——a somewhat ecclesiastical façade.

It is, necessarily, an anomalous situation. But if it is strictly inevitable might not the office and apartment remain below and the church be raised (as in the accompanying sketch) aloft?

CHURCHES ALOFT

NOT ONLY UPWARD, in skyscrapers, does the city appear forced to move, but also outward—over its bridges. At a recent meeting Architect Raymond Hood outlined the plausible possibility of utilizing the framework of bridges for apartments or offices. The idea could, of course, be visualized in various forms—in the accompanying sketch, the suspension type of bridge is assumed; the towers rise up into fifty or sixty story buildings; the serried structure between is suspended—the buildings literally hung—from cables.

At first glance it would appear that such a location for office or residence is unusually desirable as to exposure, light and air. We may naturally assume landing stages, at the bases of the towers, for launch, yacht and hydroplane—whence it would be only a minute by elevator, to one's private door.

Facetious minds have suggested that the placing of apartments in such a fashion would introduce a bizarre—not to say dangerous—element into domestic life! On the other hand, serious minds have claimed that the project is not only structurally sound but possesses unusual advantages, financially.

APARTMENTS ON BRIDGES

THE MOST FORMIDABLE RESTRAINT yet placed upon the rank growth of American building is, without doubt, the Zoning Laws which, from their experimental beginnings something over ten years ago, have already been adopted in over three hundred American municipalities.

Reference is here made especially to those provisions of the law which pertain to the height and volume of buildings. Before acceptance of the Zoning principle an owner could without let or hindrance build on his own property to any height, and in any volume, that he desired. But with continually increasing dimensions, it became apparent that the large structure could no longer be regarded as an isolated instance; it was definitely affecting adjoining buildings, the neighborhood and even the city as a whole. It became increasingly evident that the large project was a concern not only of an individual, but of the community, and that some form of restriction must be adopted.

Existing Zoning Laws now vary somewhat in different cities; the underlying principle, however, is the same, and the Law which exists in New York—and which was the pioneering example—may be regarded as typical of the trend. The accompanying drawing and those which immediately follow, though they specifically refer to the New York law, may be taken as illustrations of the effects which the Zoning principle has worked, and will continue to work, in large buildings throughout the country.

The New York law, formulated by a group of technical experts, was based on purely practical considerations. Public safety was a primary concern; by limiting the bulk of a building, the number of occupants was limited; fewer people required access and egress; traffic on adjoining streets was lightened. The limitation in mass had also of course the effect of permitting more light and air into the streets as well as into the buildings themselves. The law as a whole was directed to securing an increase in public safety, convenience, efficiency and health.

From the point of view of Design, it is interesting to recall that the Zoning movement having its genesis in just such considerations as have been mentioned was not at all inspired by concern for its possible effects on Architectural design. The recollection is interesting because the actual effect of the law was to introduce what is often spoken of as no less than a new era in American Architecture. The whole procedure constitutes another example of the fact that the larger movements of Architecture occur not as the result of some individual designer's stimulus but in response to some practical general condition.

As a matter of fact, when the Law was first passed, conservative architectural standards were thrown into confusion. At point after point designers found themselves faced by restrictions which made the erecting of familiar forms impossible.

EVOLUTION OF THE SET-BACK BUILDING—
FIRST STAGE

The writer began to speculate, shortly after the enacting of the Law, as to what effects in architectural design were imminent. He discussed the matter with several forward-looking architects and had the good fortune to find, in the diagrams which Architect Harvey Wiley Corbett was formulating, the practical basis for the first four drawings of the accompanying pictorial study.

The drawing on the preceding page is, briefly, a representation of the maximum mass which, under the Zoning Law, it would be permissible to build over an entire city block. The block is assumed to be two hundred by six hundred feet. The building rises vertically on its lot lines only so far as is allowed by law (in this case, twice the width of adjoining streets). Above this, it slopes inward at specified angles. A tower rises, as is permitted, to an unlimited height, being in area, not over one fourth the area of the property.

It must be understood that the mass thus delineated is not an architect's design; it is simply a form which results from legal specifications. It is a shape which the Law puts into the architect's hands. He can add nothing to it; but he can vary it in detail as he wishes. It is a crude form which he has to model.

THE FIRST STEP which is taken by the architect is to cut into the mass to admit light into the interior.

It must be borne in mind that the architect is not, in this case, permitting himself any prevision of his final form: there is no pet design toward which he is working. He is accepting, simply, a mass which has been put into his hands; he proposes to modify it step by step, taking these steps in logical order; he is prepared to view the progress impartially and to abide by whatever result is finally reached.

In contemplating the original mass, it was obvious that it contained great interior volumes which were inaccessible to light. He therefore cut out such portions—such "light courts"—as would admit natural light throughout. He finds remaining the form which is shown on the opposite page.

SECOND STAGE

THE FORM AS LAST SEEN still presented certain peculiarities which, from a practical point of view, are unacceptable.

There is, possibly, something about those great slopes which vaguely stirs a certain type of mind. And it has been even suggested that a sloping exterior wall could be actually built; indeed, the Foshay tower in Minneapolis bears witness. However, such decidedly sloping planes as these are alien to accepted notions of construction and demand revision. The architect, therefore, cuts into them again, this time translating them into the rectangular forms which will provide more conventional interior spaces and which can be more economically constructed in steel.

At the same time, he gives consideration to the tower. Legally, it could have risen to any height; as far as engineering limitations are concerned, it could rise considerably higher than any structure now standing. With consideration, however, for the financial aspects of the case—as well as for the other principles which evoked the zoning law, —the tower is tentatively limited to one thousand feet.

In consequence of thus translating slopes into rectangular steps, and thus limiting the tower, the mass assumes the form depicted herewith.

Upon contemplating this form, however, it is apparent that yet further revisions will be necessary. The "steps," because of their multitude and their comparatively small dimensions, would not prove an economical venture in steel; clearly, it would be better to remove those steps which do not conform to the usual simple steel grill. Also, the uppermost steps are of too small an area to be of use: when the spaces necessary for elevators and stairs has been set aside, the remaining rentable area would not justify the expense of building. These too, then, are yet to be revised.

THIRD STAGE

AFTER REMOVING THOSE PARTS which were just found to be undesirable, the mass which finally remains is that which is now illustrated. This is not intended, of course, as a finished and habitable building; it still awaits articulation at the hands of the individual designer; but it may be taken as a practical, basic form for large buildings erected under this type of Zoning Law.

What are the outstanding characteristics of this basic form? It may be seen that the limitation which the Law placed on the projected building in the first place—the spatial envelope, so to speak, into which the building must be put—is of a pyramidal character. On the other hand, we recall that practically all buildings antedating the Zoning Law were, basically, parallelogram or cube-like forms. Reducing the matter to simplest terms, we find a contrast between the pyramid and the cube.

Suppose that a number of cubes are placed side by side. (This is, in fact, what happens in the typical city block.) Each cube—that is to say, each building—loses its essential identity in the row. And each presents to the spectator in the street, not its entirety, but only one of its façades.

But no matter how closely pyramids are placed in rows, each preserves its essential individuality of form; the observer still sees, in each of them, every one of its sloping sides.

It must be added that in the pyramid there is the sense of vertical axis and the obvious apex or summit, both of which are lacking in the cube.

These simple contrasts characterize a building erected on the set-back principle. Though such a building is not, of course, a true pyramid, it is informed with certain of the pyramid's qualities. It, too, possesses that effect of individuality which is essential to architectural dignity; it exposes more than one—and usually all four—of its façades; there is, in the majority of set-back buildings, a satisfying sense of vertical axis, and in all of them one's eye is led (as it never was led in the corniced cubes) to a lofty consummation.

The effect of all this is to give back to Architecture a dimension which, in crowded metropolitan streets at least, had been lost. With the return of the third dimension, Architecture seems to resume possession of a lost glory. And if there be anything in the theory that the building affects the man in the street, we may indeed regard this architectural development as possessing human interest.

FOURTH STAGE

THE FOUR STAGES which have just been delineated, one by one, are drawn upon in this accompanying study—their characteristics being assembled, for the purposes of comparison, in the one picture.

The small form appearing in the distance, to the right, recalls the original mass which was presented on Page 73, while the other distant form suggests the mass after the sloping planes have been modelled into steps. The dark mass in the immediate foreground is, again, the mass in its fourth stage—as shown on Page 79.

But in this study, the latter mass is carried one step farther. The form which dominates this picture suggests the appearance after the exterior walls have been penetrated with the necessary window openings.

To many designers, this further step will still seem far from any final results: they seek some far greater refinement and delicacy than is here evident. To them, this form may be offered simply as a building in the rough. Yet there are designers to whom the very simplicity of such forms, the very absence of adornment, is itself a recommendation. From them we may expect buildings exhibiting a certain starkness and even nakedness—those qualities which are, indeed, the norm for all newly arisen forms.

THE FOUR STAGES

IF THE MAXIMUM MASSES which are permitted by the New York Zoning Law were erected over all the blocks of a city, an impression not unlike the one opposite would be produced.

It is understood that these are not the forms of practicable buildings; they are the embodiment of legal rather than architectural concepts; yet they indicate accurately the limits within which the designer must work——they constitute, in fact, the rough shapes with which he must deal.

As one contemplates these shapes, images may begin to form in the mind of novel types of buildings——buildings which are no longer a compilation of items of familiar styles but are, simply, the subtleizing of these crude masses.

This sketch was made with the fancy in mind that a number of such gigantic shapes were actually existing; that they were composed of clay; and that they were awaiting the hand of the sculptor.

Indeed, the crude clay of the future city may be imagined as already standing. There must come architects who, using the technique of sculptors, will model the crude clay into the finished forms.

CRUDE CLAY FOR ARCHITECTS

THE IDEA OF MODELING buildings was carried over in making the drawing opposite; the untouched shapes which appear in the previous study are here shown in various stages of the modeling process.

Mention might well be made at this point of the possible effect which the zoned building is having on the professional sculptor. In the Classic and Gothic building, the sculptor was, of course, specifically a collaborator of the architect: each of these styles of architecture evoked its corresponding style of sculptor. And we still find, in such of our modern buildings as are designed in past styles, the appropriate placements for the usual heroic or decorative figures.

But in the great set-backs which are now appearing on our larger buildings, and on their sheer planes, where will those familiar sculptures find a resting place?

It may well be that, ere long, some sculptor will conceive forms which, in scale and spirit, are at one with these new forms of architecture. Or it may be, as is here suggested, that the building in its entirety will be taken to be a sculptor's work.

BUILDINGS IN THE MODELING

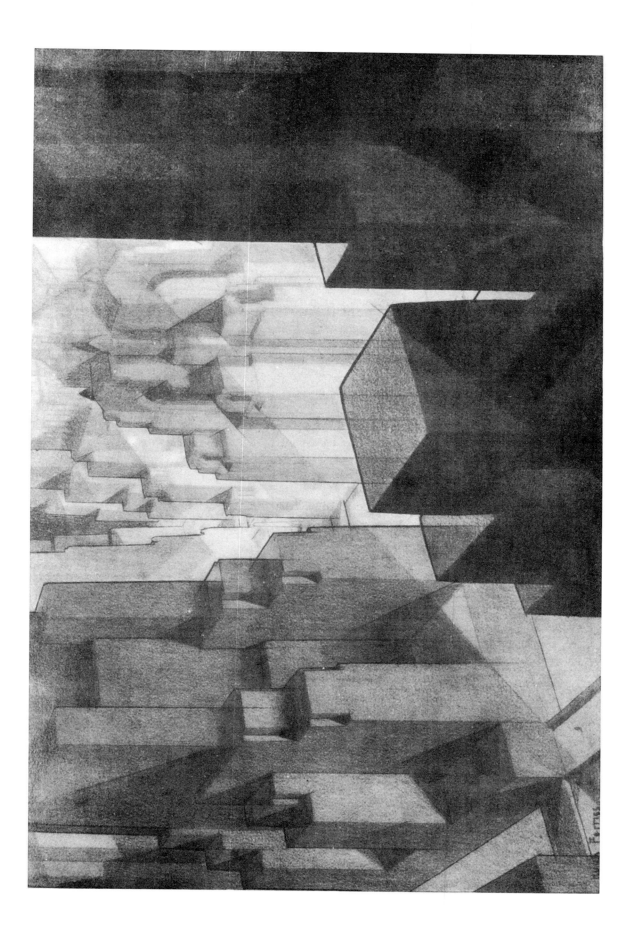

DESPITE THE ADVANTAGES of the set-back type of building, and the fact that it is being erected in great numbers throughout the country, there are designers who hold that it is not the best of all possible solutions of the problem. For example, it has been suggested that the population of a business or residence district could be more advantageously housed, and its traffic given far ampler proportions, if the buildings were required to be in the form of very high, slender towers; these would rise from comparatively small plots and would be set well apart, thus permitting wide traffic spaces between.

It would appear, indeed, that such structures would have unusual values as to exposure, light and air; but probably the greatest virtue of this proposal lies in the implied simplification of transportation. The vertical transportation is, in these narrow towers, visibly centralized, and the entire ground level, throughout the city, is made available for horizontal traffic.

VERTICALS ON WIDE AVENUES

A GROWING TENDENCY already exists to assemble larger and larger building plots when projecting tall buildings. This is partly accounted for by that provision of the Zoning Laws which permits towers to be erected on only a limited portion (in some cities, twenty-five per cent) of the ground area. If the plot is quite small, it becomes impracticable to build any tower at all; on a very large plot, a tremendous vertical can, of course, be erected.

But there are other advantages inherent in the larger real estate operation. As is now usually the case, every city block contains a considerable number of buildings, each having a different owner and each designed by a different architect. The resulting conflict (which is by no means limited to architectural design) and the waste which is involved, are really enormous. Already, we find in larger cities many buildings which cover an entire block; the result is a unity in internal functioning and in external appearance.

TWO-BLOCK BUILDING

PROJECTING THE TREND toward larger building plots, we begin to consider structures which, arching the avenue, cover two or more city blocks.

As a matter of fact, there already exist several examples of a building spanning a street. In New York alone there are the Municipal Building and the tower which strides Park Avenue just north of Grand Central Terminal.

The latter structure vividly illustrates just how fine an opportunity is presented by a tower thus located; it has become necessarily the focal point of the whole long Park Avenue vista. What an influence a strong shaft, thus located, might have exerted !

We may anticipate many other two-block buildings—thus providing the city with focal points, or architectural keynotes, which are otherwise impossible in the usual rectangular layout of city blocks.

VISTA THROUGH A TWO-BLOCK BUILDING

REVERSION TO PAST STYLES has by no means disappeared from contemporary architectural practice, despite new images inherent in Zoning Laws, despite new materials and despite the logical, and sometimes impassioned, pleas of leaders in modern design.

As a matter of fact, when the New York Zoning Law came into existence, and the new pyramid-like limitation, or "envelope," was placed over city blocks, the reaction of many architects was simply to fill this envelope with the same conventional forms with which they had always been occupied. Thus, we began to see façades, composed of the familiar base, shaft and crowning member, rising vertically from the grade as high as was permitted; where the law required the first set-back, the architect simply affixed a handsome cornice and calmly went on to repeat himself; that is to say, he started another, smaller building on top of the first, again composed of base, shaft and capital. This seemed to continue indefinitely—one "classic" building on top of another—until the total permissible volume was somehow filled.

One is scarcely in sympathy with this rather mechanical procedure; but since the author's aim in this section is to illustrate existing trends, it becomes his duty to show what would happen if architects continued piling Parthenons upon skyscrapers!

REVERSION TO PAST STYLES

THE UTILIZATION OF UPPER LEVELS, especially in the case of Apartment buildings, has been one of the interesting results of the set-back regulation. Not very long ago, the penthouse on the roof of the building contained only the elevator machinery, the tanks and, occasionally, living quarters for the janitor. The effect of stepping back the building was to draw more attention to the uppermost floor; roof spaces began to be planned on a larger scale as servants' quarters; a few adventurous individuals began to lease some of these floors, throw two or three of the diminutive rooms together and produce apartments which rather surprised their friends. The advantages which were in fact inherent in such locations—increased privacy, exposure, light and air, as well as use of an outdoor space—were increasingly appreciated; architects began to plan them in advance for use as apartments and, in course of time, realtors appreciated the point—that is to say, rents were steeply raised and, at the present moment, the erstwhile janitor's quarters have become the most expensive rentable space in the building.

The use of terraces, fortunately begun, will, without doubt, increase as time goes on, the trend leading to porticoes which will demand a greater share of the architect's attention.

LOFTY TERRACES

THE ARCHITECTURAL TREATMENT of upper levels will, doubtless, pass through many phases, romantic or extravagant, before a solution really in keeping with modern materials and contemporary requirements is achieved. We may look forward to public out-of-door gatherings, on these open terraces, of a magnitude not now possible.

Possibly some such theatrical scene as the one opposite will, for a time, meet the eye—a masked ball atop some Fine Arts building, companioned by another roof-top carnival across the avenue.

HANGING GARDENS

AGAIN IN LIGHTER VEIN we may imagine that a theatrical district——let us say, Times Square——is built up in a romantic interpretation of the Zoning Law.

The ancient Assyrian ziggurat, as a matter of fact, is an excellent embodiment of the modern New York legal restriction; may we not for a moment imagine an array of modern ziggurats, providing restaurants and theaters on their ascending levels?

MODERN ZIGGURATS

THE NEW TYPES OF GLASS, which modern ingenuity is already manufacturing, make it quite certain that before long this material will be utilized not simply as windows but as walls.

In steel construction, no specification is implied of the material that must be used for the exterior curtain walls which stand between the steel members; neither brick, stone nor terra cotta is mandatory; any practical material may be considered, and it is already evident that a glass can be produced which is a practical material.

While the thought of a glass building seems to some to be extreme, the material has, in fact, solid advantages. There is an obvious gain in natural light and (with those forms of glass which admit the ultra-violet ray) an increase in the modified rays of the sun. (A possible coöperation appears to be implied between architects and physicians.) The glass need not be visualized as transparent nor as being manufactured in the wide, thin panes now used for windows: in other words, there will not necessarily be the glass houses which invite stones. Glass has, in fact, already been produced in the form of translucent bricks—which produces an effect referred to in a later drawing rather than in the one opposite.

It has been suggested that the exterior glass wall may be built of a double thickness (the building thus becoming a sort of thermos bottle); that totally new types of window shades, or screens, may be developed: and that the glass may be made in various colors.

GLASS

CONCRETE, while impractical for the extremely tall structure, may be used, in the near future, for buildings considerably higher than at present.

The accompanying study was made as an interpretation of the New York Zoning Law in terms of this material. Basically, it is the same form as was developed on Page 79; but the mass is here simply carried farther by indication of the solids and voids which seemed practicable in concrete.

CONCRETE

STEEL will, without doubt, continue to be the structural material for strong buildings for many years to come. It is true that we have been erecting tall structures with it for only a very few decades and we cannot yet claim to be thoroughly familiar with its properties. There are occasional rumors of its permanency being less certain than is yet realized; and there already are suggestions of improved metal substitutes.

In the accompanying study, however, the continued use of steel is taken for granted. Here are also brought together several other of the contemporary trends which have been referred to: the stepping back of buildings along lines of the New York Zoning Law, the utilization of more than one city block as bases for longer structures and ever increasing altitudes.

STEEL

AN IMAGINARY METROPOLIS

PART THREE

LET US RETURN to the parapet which provided us with our original bird's-eye view of the existing city. It is again dawn, with an early mist completely enveloping the scene. Again, there lies beneath us, curtained by the mist, a Metropolis—and the curtain, again, is about to rise. But, in this case, let us have it rise, not on the existing city, but on a city of the imagination.

As the mists begin to disperse, there come into view, one by one, the summits of what must be quite lofty tower-buildings; in every direction the vistas are marked by these pinnacles as far as the eye can reach. It is apparent that this city, like those with which we had been previously familiar, contains very tall buildings and very many of them; indeed, we may assume, from their dimensions and their disposition over so wide an area, that here is an even greater center of population than anything we had hitherto known.

At the same time, however, we are struck by certain peculiarities in the disposition of the towers now before us. In the first place, no two of them rise in close juxtaposition to each other; roughly calculated, they appear in no case to be less than half-a-mile apart. Also, there is a certain degree of regularity apparent in their disposal throughout; while they are not all precisely equidistant, and their relation does not suggest an absolutely rectangular checkerboard scheme, yet it is obvious that they have been located according to some city-wide plan.

A little later, the general clearing of the scene allows us to check up our first impressions. The tower-buildings rise to a height of a thousand feet from the ground—in a few particular cases, yet higher. And we now see that they spring from very broad bases, as well: their foundations cover three or four city blocks. In the particular cases mentioned, they must cover six or eight blocks.

Yet, in the wide districts which lie between these towers—and which make up by far the greater area of the city—the buildings are all comparatively low. They average six stories; that is to say, they are no higher than the width of the streets which they face. Looking directly down upon the roofs of these buildings, we distinguish a color which suggests the presence of an abundance of planting.

The first confirmed impression of the city is thus of a wide plain, not lacking in vegetation, from which rise, at considerable intervals, towering mountain peaks.

This arrangement does not, indeed, embody any zoning principle which is altogether strange to us; obviously the zoning laws of this city, in so far as they pertain to heights and volumes of buildings, are reminiscent of other laws, previously encountered, which permitted a tall tower only over a certain percentage of a given area. In this case, the minimum area which may contain a tower is simply greater and the percentage of that area which the tower may cover is smaller. And yet, although no novel or difficult legal conception is involved and although this disposition of greater towers at greater intervals indicates simply an increase in dimensions, it is this very magnification in the scale which produces results—both practical and æsthetic—which are in decided contrast to cities previously seen.

The cities with which we were previously familiar may, in a given area, compare as to total cubic content with the city now below us. In other words, a great number of typical, fairly large skyscrapers, set in very close juxtaposition, may have the same total cube, and house the same population as a few tremendous towers set at wide intervals—with very low buildings in the intervening areas.

In the former cases, however, the close juxtaposition of formidable masses—the monotonous repetition of similar bulks for block after city block—the close store of equally high façades across narrow streets,—all combine to shut the human being away from air, light, and every pleasing prospect. In the city now below us—the same cubic content is so disposed, and high masses so dispersed, that a more humane environment seems possible.

Let us now note, in the particular disposition of the masses at present before us, a possible æsthetic gain (not forgetting however, what has already been indicated more than once, that the psychological aspect is of interest because of its practical results). The fact is that in the general run of cities, the tall individual skyscraper, however, well designed can very seldom be individually seen. That is to say, juxtaposition is so close that only bits of the structure can be seen at one time by the pedestrian. Only by craning the neck does one see the whole of a tower; and then, of course, one sees only a ridiculous distortion. But in the city, now before us, each great mass is surrounded by a great spaciousness; here, we may assume, the citizen's habitual prospects are ample vistas. Without altering his upright posture, his glance may serenely traverse the vista and find at its end a dominating and upright pinnacle.

*   *   *   *

Let us scrutinize the streets. The eye is caught by a system of broad avenues which must be two hundred feet wide and which are placed about half a mile apart. One notes that it is precisely at the intersections of these avenues that the tower buildings rise. We may conclude that here is a system of superhighways which carry the express traffic of the city and that the tower buildings are express stations for traffic.

The half-mile-wide districts which are bounded by these highways are themselves traversed by streets of much lesser width—scarcely more than sixty feet; obviously, they are planned to carry only the traffic which is local to the district.

On restudying these low-lying districts together with the occasional tower buildings, it appears that the latter are not to be compared simply to mountain formations which happen to have arisen, abruptly and at certain intervals, in a plain; rather, each tower seems to have a specific relation to the low-lying district which immediately surrounds it. The heights of the lesser buildings increase as they approach the central tower; each peak, so to speak, is surrounded by foothills.

It would seem that each of these formations—each peak together with its slopes and contributory plain—forms a sort of unit. Those units may indicate that the city is zoned not only as to height but as to use (which, again, would be a familiar principle) and that some particular activity, some specific function of the whole municipal body, is carried on in each unit.

A question arises, incidentally, as to these tower buildings. They are very tall, and cover enormous ground areas; each must house a multitudinous activity; each stands in a considerable isolation from other buildings of the same species; each dominates, and is, we may assume, the center of control of a particular district. Is the word "building" any longer sufficiently definitive? For the sake of simplicity, let us adopt for them the term "center."

Looking off to the right from our parapet, we distinguish a group of these centers which seem larger than the rest. They stand together about a large open space; they seem to constitute a sort of nucleus of the city—perhaps they are its primary centers. Let us turn our binoculars in that direction.

THE FIRST CENTER to be seen is that structure, or complex of structures, in which the control of the business activities of the city is housed. Here is located the seat of government of the city's practical affairs, including its three chief branches—legislative, judiciary and executive.

At this closer view we can distinguish in greater detail the characteristics of the tower-buildings. The tower itself rises directly over the intersection of two of the master highways to a height of 1200 feet. There are eight flanking towers, half this height, which, with their connecting wings, enclose four city blocks. The center extends, however, over eight adjoining blocks, where its supplementary parts rise to a height of twelve stories.

We see, upon examining the Avenue, that more than one level for traffic is provided. Local wheel traffic is on the ground level; express traffic is depressed; pedestrians pass on a separate plane above.

Beyond the center, the lower districts of the city are visible, together with the radial avenues which lead to the other tower-buildings of the Business district.

THE BUSINESS CENTER

THE SECOND STRUCTURE TO BE OBSERVED is the Art center. Situated about a mile from the Business center, it is also one of the group of major centers which first drew our attention.

By taking up a viewpoint nearer to the ground level, we see more definitely how the longer structures of the city tower above the great majority of the buildings.

Presumably there is, in such an architectural landscape, a free access to light and air on the part of all buildings, whether high or low.

A distinct advance has been accomplished in this imaginary city in the matter of smoke elimination: the roofs of all the lower structures have been developed into sun porches and gardens. The fact is, there is two feet of soil on these roofs, and trees are generally cultivated. Open-air swimming pools are frequent.

THE ART CENTER

AT SOME DISTANCE from the two structures which have just been viewed we find the Science center.

Here again is a very high central mass, supported by large wings, the whole extending over adjoining streets to embrace outlying structures.

Here is housed control of the scientific activities of the city; these structures being planned on a large scale for laboratory work and scientific research.

The traffic plane is wide and calculated to carry a great number of vehicles on more than one level. A waterway is carried down the axis of the main avenue.

THE SCIENCE CENTER

THE THREE CENTERS which have just been seen constitute the nucleus, the group of primary centers, which originally drew our attention from our distant balcony.

We must now note that each of these centers dominates a very wide district; that is to say, the city is divided into a Business zone, an Art zone and a Science zone.

Let us descend into the Business zone. This, naturally, is the largest of the three districts. We find that its tower-buildings rise to greater heights; that they are closer together; and that the master highways have been developed for the maximum traffic.

VISTA IN THE BUSINESS ZONE

THE BUSINESS ZONE is again seen in the accompanying view. In this case, we are looking west; the Business center is in the foreground,—its relation with adjoining tower-buildings appearing from a somewhat different angle than on Page 113.

IN THE ART ZONE, as in the Business zone, we find tower-buildings only at considerable intervals. Here, however, more ground space is left open, and the main avenues are to a great extent parked.

VISTA IN THE ART ZONE

BUILDINGS like crystals.
Walls of translucent glass.
Sheer glass blocks sheathing a steel grill.
No Gothic branch: no Acanthus leaf: no recollection of the plant world.
A mineral kingdom.
Gleaming stalagmites.
Forms as cold as ice.
Mathematics.
Night in the Science Zone.

NIGHT IN THE SCIENCE ZONE.

THE POWER PLANT is located at the base of the Business zone. In this city, coal is still being used; it is carried aloft, from the cars, on the inclined elevators and stored in the uppermost of the three levels of the building. From here it is lowered to the boilers on the second level. The structure is built of concrete.

POWER

THROUGHOUT EACH ZONE of the city, we find numerous tower-buildings which are related, by master highways, to the major center.

These minor centers, or sub-centers, are each the headquarters of some particular department of the general activity of the zone. For example, we find in the Business zone the rather large structure which serves as the Financial center.

Each of these tower-buildings houses all the facilities for the day's work; containing, in addition to the offices themselves, the necessary post office, bank, shops, restaurants, gymnasiums and so on. Each is, so to speak, a city in itself.

FINANCE

THE RELATION OF TOWER TO STREET is shown in more detail in the present view—which happens to be of the Technology center. The ground level, practically in entirety, is given over to wheel traffic; parking is all beneath the buildings. The avenue has also a lower level, in the center, which is used by express wheel traffic. We glimpse, through the openings in the retaining wall of this lower level, the right-of-way of the subway rail traffic.

In the design of this building, by the way, one may note an emphasis on the horizontal lines, rather than the vertical lines, of the steel grill. It may be questioned whether designers can, logically, emphasize either, when both are essential in this system of construction. The horizontal emphasis, at least, recognizes and makes permanent the appearance which, in actuality, the steel building itself always exhibits before the exterior walls have been added.

In this particular building, the vertical members contain the elevator shafts and fire stairs.

TECHNOLOGY

A LOFT BUILDING, in the Industrial Arts district, is here viewed just before the glass exterior walls have been constructed. The latter will scarcely change the visual impression produced by the steel grill itself: that is to say, we see here the actual horizontals which were taken as the cue for the finished design of the Technology center.

INDUSTRIAL ARTS

IN THE CITY which is momentarily before us, the many and varied religious denominations have achieved—for that moment!—a state of complete harmony: the building now in view is none other than the seat of their combined and coordinated activities.

Expressive of modern tendencies, this structure soars to great altitudes; if it has, at the same time, a slightly medieval cast, this is perhaps not altogether inexpressive of the institution which it domiciles.

Even in the sharp perspective of the present view, one may surmise the presence of three outstanding towers—the two lesser being toward either end of the mass and the lofty central tower rising between. These stand, respectively, for the cardinal functions of this Christian host: one of the flanking towers houses the executive offices of the various Faiths; the other is more especially dedicated to their aspirational activities, or Hopes; in the third, which is the greatest of these, abide the Charities.

RELIGION

WHERE ART AND SCIENCE MEET—that is to say, where these civic zones contact with one another,—there stands a tower about which are gathered the colleges of Arts and Sciences.

Since this tower seems to stand somewhat apart, let us give a moment to examining the particular elements of its design.

In plan, it seems to show, at all levels, variations of a nine-pointed star—in other words of three superimposed triangles. Being planned, basically, on the equilateral triangle, the shaft rises—or, so to speak, grows—in what seem definite stages. For example, the vertical dimension from the top of the base up to the point where the vertical members break for the first time appears to bear a ratio to the dimension between this break and the break next above it, as well as to the total vertical dimension above the latter break. These three dimensions are to each other as three, one and three. (This could be actually measured, of course, only in a direct elevation and can be only inferred from this perspective presentation).

This ascension in a total of seven units must perhaps be regarded as purely arbitrary; we can only affirm that this relationship which appears in the total form appears also in its lesser parts; for example, the last and uppermost of the three divisions just referred to, is itself broken vertically into three parts in which the original ratio repeats. Indeed this particular kind of "growth" appears to continue upward indefinitely.

The real significance, if any, of a tower having, so to speak, a threefold plan and a sevenfold ascension, is obscure. And it is perhaps optimistic to say that here a number of separate parts aspire to be as one. In any case, this is the Center of Philosophy.

PHILOSOPHY

TO CONSTRUCT A DETAILED MAP of a panorama which is only momentarily before us would scarcely be practicable; but, as a result of even a brief bird's-eye view, we can sketch a general layout of the city plan. It will give us a clearer notion of how the traffic arteries are disposed and how the buildings are zoned as to height and use.

We may first note, in this sketch plan, the black spots which indicate location of the tower-buildings, as well as the broad light lines of the main avenues; in short, the centers and the circulating system which connects them.

Let us take as a point of departure, the structure which is upon the circumference of the central circle (which is letter "1" on the plan). This is the Business center of the city—that complex of buildings which was glimpsed on Pages 113 and 121. The circular area upon whose edge it stands is the principal open space of the city: the Civic Circle which, with its parks, playgrounds and areas for open-air gatherings and exhibitions, is the focal point to which the radial avenues lead. It is likewise the fountain-head of the waterways which distribute throughout the smaller parks of the city.

The district which lies below the Business center as well as to the right and left of it—in other words, that whole third of the plan which is penetrated by the avenues radiating from this center—constitutes the Business zone of the city. Here, in close proximity to the center, are located, in tower-buildings, the headquarters of the various principal business activities and, grouped about them, the chief industrial sub-centers.

At a distance of a mile or so from the Business center, the airports can be noted, located on the main radial avenues, as well as the beginning of the outlying residential districts. The latter appear as the shaded areas which are pointed toward the center of the city and which increase in width as they extend, fan-wise, outward. It is apparent that both the business zone and the residential districts which flank it may expand indefinitely away from the Civic Circle. Such expansion, however, must be along the radial lines which will, in all events, continue to relate added outlying districts to the center.

Returning to the Civic Circle, we find indication of another large structure upon the circumference (lettered "2" on the plan). This is the Art center which was sketched on Page 115. As in the case of the Business zone, radial lines extend outward from this center, constituting the arterial system of the Art zone. Here are located the tower-buildings in which center such civic activities as the Drama, Music, Architecture and so on.

The third structure upon the circumference of the Civic Circle is the Science center (lettered "3") which, like the two former, occupies a dominating position in relation to the zone behind it.

In addition to the radial avenues which have been mentioned and which connect

EPILOGUE

WE HAVE ALREADY spent too long a time in contemplation of what is only a mirage. The curtain of mist quickly reenvelops such momentary scenes; we must return again—and at once—to less shadowy spectacles and less theoretical proposals: in short, to the City of Today.

Let us only repeat, as we leave this parapet, what we said at the very outset. Architecture influences the lives of human beings. City dwellers react to the architectural forms and spaces which they encounter: specific consequences may be looked for in their thoughts, feelings and actions. Their response to Architecture is usually subconscious. Designers themselves are usually unconscious of the effects which their creations will produce. Nevertheless, we may look forward to some stirring of thought—perhaps even to some specific training—which will put a considerable body of students in command of the architectural Influence. Our criterion for judging this self-conscious Architecture will be its effect on human values: its net contribution to the harmonious development of man. We hope that eventually it will not only adequately meet the demands of our physical welfare, but will also serve in actualizing whatever may be man's potentialities of emotional and mental well-being.

Who, indeed, can specifically define these potentialities—and what architects can prepare contributory or evocative designs? It may well be that at the present moment there are none; nor will there be, until architects have begun to call into their draughting rooms the scientist, the psychologist, the philosopher . . .

For the present, we shall have done well, if we have sketched, in any firm line, a really adequate objective for the general work of city planning. As for personal and specific proposals—the author well knows how many parapets, other than the one we are now leaving, overlook the imaginary "Metropolis of Tomorrow" and he shares the common belief that few of the many visualizations currently being formulated can contribute more than a particle to the ultimate actuality. Concerning the "threefold city" which has just been outlined, he has indeed but one word to add:

A few years ago, he happened upon a rather curious inscription. The manuscript was partly mutilated; it may have been of quite ancient origin. Was it simply a curio? Or did it contain a clue? The author did not actually comprehend . . . yet he secured the copy which he now, at the last moment, includes—leaving it to whatever attention the chance reader may be inclined to give. . . .

THE CITY

ITS SCIENCES   ITS ARTS

ITS BUSINESS

COULD BE MADE IN THE IMAGE OF

MAN

HIS THOUGHTS   HIS FEELINGS

HIS SENSES

WHO IS MADE IN THE IMAGE OF